WOLF
HAT
IRON
SHOES

Poems | Martha McCollough

LILY POETRY REVIEW BOOKS

For my parents, in memory

Contents

WOLF
HAT
IRON
SHOES

Plague Diary

I'm living by owl's hours
nowhere to be but
this bed my workshop

who can think in the dark
or love a morning grey
with threat of late snow

still the peepers go
about their frantic business
as in other years

outside the back door
a disheveled garden springs
up of its own sweet will

Full Flower Moon

in old plague times   you'd drop your coin
        in a bowl of vinegar
this morning the drugstore clerk
        holds out his offertory basket
                broomstick taped to a plastic bin
    dread runs a light finger   down the back
                        of your neck
        later rain comes down hard
            on a speechless evening

cut hyacinth opening in a glass
        sweet but with undertones of death
like a saint's miraculous corpse   you wouldn't say
                    it looked *fresh*, exactly
        around it the shrine grown old   a little dank
            mystery of sameness in time
        in a church where no one believes
                where candles lit by tourists
                have smoked the tintoretto ceiling
            surely by now the reliquary gems
                are secretly glass

studying her crystal   the fortune teller
        sees such a little way   into futurity
        she says undertones of death   coy of course
on details   like just exactly who what
and how the rest will know it's time   to creep ftom their dens
        reappear   like angels   bleached of experience
            damp-winged and blinking
                    in the uncomfortable light
                    of strangers' eyes
in their glass jar
the hyacinths stand at attention   until suddenly
            they flop   neck-broken
                lord how vain are all our frail delights

2

Spring Moon

my mind turns and turns
    a restless dog   uneasy in the warm room
    wanting to chase the moon
        to roll in starlit mud
        splash in puddles   get filthy
            to meet other strays by the pond
           in moonlight   to howl together
                    to follow coyotes
        to observe the owl
        hunting in silence
my mind is tired
of turning over symptoms
        of telling the frightened body
        go to sleep   it's nothing
           nothing   it will be morning soon

All these omens

comets and a crowing hen
antichrist squatting
      in the seat of power.

the century's logo:
      goofball dog in a hat
      red tongue
            dangling sideways
      X X for its eyes

trash fire burning
mid street

is this fine

maybe long oblivion can
erase our embarrasment or do I mean shame

I mean
can *you* tell the ostrogoths
         from the visigoths
         or keep the dull presidents straight
no
just throw us what's-his-name
the emperor's   head
in a basket

wild spring
I wish I were with you
        floating like smoke
          through teargas streets

you said
as the dream of every cliché   is to enter a poem
the dream of every lie   is to slither into history

above us
all the home-come chickens
            weigh the branches into downward arcs
            every tree in the park weeping

Reading The Roaring Stream

to him his lice and his followers are about the same

1
the louse is a nightmare   so is a moth body
seen close up   & the spider traversing the screen door
                    is a tiny black crab who expected
                        to be born into a bigger life

the mayfly may cling to my sleeve I give it permission
slender green needle   exhausted by its winged summer

I spray the doorframes   with sweet orange   lavender
        patchouli (it is good for something)
        ten drops each in water
            to keep houseflies at bay   though i have
                        no other companions

what loneliness said
about a spider
company's company, after all

I'm nearly there
so thin   my ghost
has grown   so thin

2
once crowds   birds or people   gathered around
        a fallen loaf of bread   a violin
            as if there were nothing to fear

3
half in a stone bowl hollowed out
by endless water pouring down the ledges

water striders skate on thready legs
tiny black fish hover at my knee

an escaping word   the mind pursues
        minnow   flickering in the shallows
            slipping through fingers

the water buoys me up
        briefly birdlike
                I float above
                the green valley

does this little mountain
have a name

History

Last box of black apples. Time to know a small number
of things very well—half fox in a fable, half handyman.
I am prepared to be bored though I'm told it's a spiritual
crime. You get used to a limited winter diet, rutabagas
and television. Contrary to expectation things continue
to happen. Tornado, wildfire, wars, chipping away.
Angel blown backward in the storm. I want an apple
red all the way through, an apple that understands sin. I
go into the orchard on a frozen morning, pick an empty
ice apple. Smell of grass rising in the thaw, the wreckage
piling up, sharp bits falling off, clinking, all the way
from Eden.

The Museum

A dry weaverbird's nest
                strung from a branch
least weasel
        & wolverine   red stilt-legged wolf

spotted clouded striped
                snarl of predators
a rearing herd
        midflight   heavy antlered elk

in a dim room the jerboa's
            little matchgirl ribs

lone glass bee   thirsty
            among so many flowers.

frayed fawn curled   in its glass case
        in its air of alertness   in its pale twist of grass

Half Light

a live owl looking at me
through green twigs

another thought
behind my thought

clings to our shared
three seconds of now

thought and thought-of
flick and jitter

pursuing what flees
to the desert of next

call it *life of the mind*
more useless than my cat

back and forth
rabbit, duck, rabbit

what has been
what is now given

name still in the book
the creature gone

Pyjama Catshark

one
of the minor
sharks

small, harmless

how it responds
to threat:
curls in circle
hiding eyes with tail

lalala pyjama catshark
can't see you

sinking down
and down
into blue
silence

called cat
for its slit-pupilled eyes

pyjama for the stripes
in which it lies

motionless
all day

like a
depressed
writer

in its
weedy
bed

Cacoethes

the hero always says
one more job and I'm done

having left the house—
what is the word
for that regret

she (the hero) longs
to be lost in her labyrinth

dodging shady minotaurs
reeling up loose threads

longs to be harmless
to live on grass or on light

but the nights
are too long
the air smells burnt

like dusty radiators
her gun hand itches

she needs to be
out in the storm
driving anywhere

where the car dies
she'll stay

like Zatoichi
like Johnny Guitar

Her Lair

she's worldwide
can see all of the road
through owlish eyes

she can tell the stars
from the chickens
you better believe it

she finds a beehive
she whispers
wake up   everyone's gone

bees hurl themselves
down the sweet field
into the blue clover

the worldwide hero
can see all the stars
from her control room

open to the sky
a humming
a glass dome

Him Again

the old hero arrives
    like any catastrophe
        one more
           in a series of disasters

he was bound to show up
    behind the dragon or ogre
        vested at first with a certain glamor
        a man without fear

but soon you start to feel judged
    and by this musclehead!
        it's nearly as awkward
           as having a saint in town

as for the ladies
    sometimes he takes one up
        like pocketing a shiny dime in the driveway

On Setting Out: words from the crone by the side
of the road

be bold be bold but not too bold

take half a loaf
and a blessing

you won't get far
in *those* shoes

by root mutter
by owl rise
by flittermouse

the right wood
to be lost in

turn left
disappear

always some wreck of a castle
a desolation at the margins

you'll have a task: to spin or sort
or visit hell for a glass of Lethe

put on your wolf hat
pretend the yellow glass eyes
are your own unreadable eyes

you won't emerge
unchanged

the ogre comes rumbling—
jump on his horse and run

throw down
the comb of flames
the comb of floods

take the talking goose
if it wants to go

Psyche

clattering
a bad stealaway
my iron shoe
cracks the walk

discarded half coin
lamp spatter
whose perverse
spell is this

night hovers
no spangled
coloratura but
cold indigo

monopoly moon
fugitive apparition
shine down on us
discontinued tokens

thimble or tin dog
never to pass go
ride the railroad
own a street

the iron staff
rusted to filigree
inside the cloud
a rush of feathers

Penelope Unweaving

night erases
these geese
my guests
my little flock
rows of sleepers
faint as ghosts
the cats catch
at loose threads
stealth unpicks
a leaf a stripe
a knotted wreath
the tight rows
ravel into flags
madder and lake
fretting the weft
by thin light
of dish moon
nail moon
potato moon
rose curls to bud
spirals to the root
to a russet hip
king in the dirt
harassed
by sparrows
midnight renews
the pluck and tug
my unwork
my calendar
my wine dark
wave undone
the little ship
a black thread
wound on
wooden spool

Erinys

do you hear
that voice
outsmarting
itself again

saying saying
makes it so

send a green fly
to annoy
send a black fly
for torment

from your cave
doorway to hell
my heart
or whatever

hell of boredom
or lake of fire

in which love
falls apart
click click
nothing

consider
the history
of love

how there is
so little of it

humming black
cloud in the shape
& place of me

be in the world
visit his sleep

Hey, Sailor

a row of black lamps
anxious creak & splash

past my archipelago
of flowers, of bones

bleaching in meadows
under the moon's frown

if I flutter skull to skull
it's my ladybird nature

to sing & have claws—
a voice kinder than home

suspended in
the sweetest overdose

Andromeda

a little star becomes a starry wheel
        rolling in huge silence   toward us
announced by meteoric children
        flashing to nobody's rescue
the catastrophe
will be continuous
      too big to be felt

thinking   *I don't want to*
the bride approaches glittering
      speechless

later she'll wonder   must every
        wedding be a bloodbath

spidersilk plus cosmic debris equals
       cobweb veil of andromeda
     spiraling from interplanetary cloud
        down to her rock
brightly particulate
in slanted light
    dust in the clouded eye
        of told you so
eye that sees
    mother trail bright waves
      across her wrist   *no one*
        more beautiful   all mothers
say these things   but mother not
where the gods can hear

that's how you end up wheeling
    upside down   through heaven
       nailed to your glittery throne

clink of chains
andromeda's monster rises
    where the sea roars & whitens
        time for the sacred wedding
or feast
perhaps the god thinks
it will be a treat for him

but what can he do, Cetus
    with this breathing thing
        finless   earthy   no part
          of his usual diet

someone should ask if he might rather
        sink   silent as the bride
          into the starless deep

. . .

  already andromeda
    shone like a dropped
      earring
      over the departures
        of certain huge animals
      slow-moving   dusty as old rugs
    leaving a bitter remnant
      wild cousins missing
        their phantom familiars

osage orange   honeylocust   coffeetree
  all this puzzling unsweetness
    is fidelity
        to the austere preference
        of vanished monsters

apple will you stay sweet
    without your bees
        your bears   gorging on windfall
          in abandoned orchards
what is a word for
    animals that wish

. . .

she wishes for
    a winged bridegroom
      spiraling down
   meteoric flash of his shield
eyes closed   waving the fatal head
   he'll say don't look
      and she won't

The Gods

Vague heads rubbed away on old coins.. Pale as a faded curtain. Is there a god concealed among the folds. I thought not. Weightless, inconsequent. No one remembers what they're supposed to be good for. Shifters of consequence. Worn out, the gods climbed into a book. Now no one remembers those transformations of mercy or casual spite. The book sleeps in the library, musty with age.

Like this like that

flame in slow motion curls
& ripples like yellow silk

braids & unbraids like water
splashing down jagged rocks

even now I can hardly
tell things one from another
or myself from the rest of it—

to put on my flame
yellow dress doesn't
burn even a little—

from the eye a mild fire
reaches out to caress
the untrustworthy world

bring back reports
to the little king enthroned
in the court of my skull—

explaining veils, barfights
the pressure of gaze

flame, ink, apples
a crow bleeding
into fresh snow

the little king looks
out on the snow

wants a child
like this like that

Self Portrait in a Pathless Garden

blue orchard bees
geometer moth
splendid fairy wren
all out of place
but the gardener
cultivates a taste
for disorder
for stinging insects
& the wanton vine
hedges gnawed
by winter deer
into starving shapes
cattail & wild carrot
a useless harvest
she's weaving straws
into her straw-pale hair

Tree shadows

cross the road
like cracks in the real.

Lying on cold grass
we look at the stars,

wait for the galaxy's
dim cross-section

to fade in behind
bright constellations.

Our eyes follow faint
light into a giddy sense

of falling up into the sky
in a night full of noise—

small rackety things
shrill on the edges

of this field not thinking
of time or orphan light.

Scale

Here at the edge
of the Milky Way
everyone's got a poem
on dying stars, on seeing
the light of the past

how if your telescope
were only strong enough
you could see time begin

if it weren't
for the dust

we've all seen sections of night
packed with a zillion galaxies
falling back and back

you start to think
an angel's wing brushing
a rock ten miles across
once every hundred years
until it wears away
is a thing you can get a grip on

like moths
writing poems
about the moon

Many Worlds Theory

In the garden the ranunculus you pick or don't pick doubles
its twisty green curl and soft rosette. There are so many
better versions of you: prettier (took care of their nails, wore
sunblock), smarter, and also a flipbook of monsters. One or
more are eaten by a bear or bears, one is a forger, one loves
a good conspiracy. Each is a leaf shivering on the tree of
yourself, as many as the grains of sand along as many Ganges
as there are grains of sand along—sorry—I mean to say a
complex rose of alt.yous exiled in the instant of becoming.
All the way down the long fall of double and vanish

If time is a dimension like space is everything still here somewhere

I can say the words *sand, wavelet, soft chill,* but I've lost the hour of wading in the lake's margin. I can still hear my grandmother, though, saying I *might* be pretty, someday. A stab to the heart, Grandma. Oh slings, oh arrows. Where/when is the golden age? Under the green lichened branches of the maple tree, in the drift of pollen on the table. Before we were born. Or now, but elsewhere. This might be the age of suffering. For animals, hell. The gods are fighting the demigods, who want their infinity pools and vanity rocketships. Their excellent plastic surgeons. Everything real at once. That's how it is.

Black Hole Diary

dear X
lately I spend my time in the study of black holes and by study
I mean watching all the youtube animations I can find and then
free associating

I've learned:

beyond the event horizon of a black hole
time is ((((ffffrozen))))

a black hole swallows a star
like a dog drinking from a garden hose

. . .

the internet asks an astrophysicist:
what color is absence
can dark matter give you powers
backwards happen can time if what
you might think these questions were from children
but no it's all 42-year-old men

. . .

meanwhile my niece dreams of a black hole under the bed and is
afraid / I say don't worry they just evaporate / which seems to be true
but will take about as long as all the time there is / I leave that out

not coming for us
black holes don't roam
the galaxy like roaring lions
seeking stray suns to devour
despite their lurid press

. . .

dear X
we might think of the cosmos as a giant circus:

    for example   a black hole is a clown car but the clowns can't get out.
    for example   space is a bouncy castle whose center is everywhere
    for example   gravity is a midway barker
               charismatic lowlife reeling you in
               roll up, roll up   to a tent full of trapped curiosities

this morning I saw you   time   lean against the door of the leopard
cage   sway the door a little back and forth   the leopards up on their
hind legs staring over your shoulders   their eyes like suns

does all of space taste of gunpowder

fleeing stars we also flee

. . .

dear X
I have accidentally swallowed a black hole / I'm full of darkness / disap-
pearing / waving goodbye goodbye

. . .

the sky is crowded with animals
       it is a cabinet of clocks and bears
            beneath these
                  the astronomer's pet telescope
            floats weightless
                  delicate wings
                     unfurled to light

the universe reels
around my house
drunk and happy

the stars bounce and roll
on the huge imaginary

      speeding   asleep

say why the wind of the turning planet doesn't knock us down
say why the wind from the sun doesn't lift my hair

Then

You can tell it's the past because I'm lighting a
cigarette off a cigarette / and no one is building
condos in the fields along the harbor / because there
are only tall grass, a broken shopping cart, a hawk
hopping after mice / what I miss about the past:
smoking and uselessness

Angel

the witness angel in the oak / watches a crow row
through milk-mild air / hears pigs below rooting for
acorns / sees vetch leap a ditch in slow motion / all
day long the wild bees forage / at dusk the cautious
deer step out of the thicket

Not Working

work is our
punishment

and because I
am not sorry

I mean to do
as little
as possible

eye adrift
like Redon's
ominous balloon

looking
at nothing or the wall
with great intensity

I want to see
what the cat sees

insect ghosts
jitter of molecules

between dust motes
into some elsewhere

that might be
heaven though

no one here
cares to find out

Jerome in the Wilderness

In a God's-eye
view all the edges
are sharp

Tiny but distinct
Jerome
picnics on a ledge
with his apocryphal lion
sunlight falling
on him in particular

does he wonder
if God might prefer him
unwashed
in stained starving rags
as he has recommended
to the Roman matrons
some now (presumably)
in heaven but no

he's wearing rose silk
he's brought along his tall crucifix,
a skull, the egg-shaped
stones he likes—
the elegant apparatus
of his project

his hat's a red bright
circle on the grass

behind him
from a stony spindle
green hills
tumble to the horizon

there is
so much to see

the light
that burnishes
the sawtooth
edge of every leaf

small castles
punctuating the wilderness

and in a corner
awkward camels
crossing a narrow bridge

the lion
dozes

Jerome
kneeling half out
of his robe
holds up a stone

ready to hit himself
and to go on hitting

hard

until God pays
attention

Apophenia

blinding brightness kicks
you off your mule lights
up your skeleton
the afterglow crackles
in your teeth gives
you that anti-charisma
later an angel nails
a page to the inside
of your skull
a to-do list
you're done now
with sleep
the cloud shredding
against your razored
halo—don't ask
is that god or a wish—
eliding inevitable
suffering of strangers
of children of animals
you insist the things
resemble the words
you have laid out

Water from Mars

it's enough
   to know it exists

trickling down
   the red bluff

leaving a glaze
   of strange salts
      across the sand

so if you were planning
   to launch a rocket crowned
      with an empty glass

or somehow dream
   yourself there
      and home again—

oh now you tell me
   you tell me

hiding the murky bottle
   behind your back

Kawaii Killer

Sorry
very sorry

I'm sorry I shot you
with my hello kitty gun

I know
it's copyright infringement

but c'mon
isn't it so so cute

I mean look
each hello kitty
holds a hello kitty gun
covered with hello kitties

I hear their murmurs

infinite regression
of expressionless
adorable kitties
whispering
shoot

War Movie

in the street Team Giant Eagle
is fighting Team Fresh City
for the potable water

neighbor please
don't shoot

at night
out comes everyone
whose job it is to be terrible

in the ruins of the Lock'n'Load
Bait & Ammo Shop
Polyphemos wrestles John Galt
for the last Kalashnikov

here we go
all against all against all

fired from a cartoon cannon
a head hurtles
into a red abyss,

deflating thought balloon
still whispering *have mercy!*
abyss still whispering *no*

Flight

the soundtrack is less
blackbird whistle

more helicopters
womping overhead

surely the times
call for fire

when I was a child, refugees
fled through old newsreels:

bundled, lumpy
with small valuables

pushing wheelbarrows
down burning winter streets

toward some border or small town
where one has a cousin

now it's half the world
in the transit of drowning and fire

we are already pacing
the chilly waiting room

hoping to be awake when
this is fine turns into *get out now*

A bad end

the bad things you've done pursue you / in the form of
a fabulous beast / whose mouth is the entrance to hell /
crashing through wood and thicket you reach and cling
to the door of your house gasping / as though it could save
you from something dense as the earth's core / thing for
which walls hardly exist

Little House in the Forest of Giant Ferns

faint fiddle music
along green aisles

your bones vibrate
to a note bowed on
the deepest string

otherwise only
soft insect hum
clicking carapace

of giant scorpion
or millipede deep
in the shady grove

there was or will
be a prairie a big
wood a creek bank

ghost pa's in the parlor
playing *boil that*
cabbage down

Life List

raven loves a good updraft
rising and dropping

keeping his eye
on the desirable
sandwiches

he knows
we know
he's watching
. . .

According to this
or that folkloric source
    birds can be understood
    at night after one has eaten
        a particular fruit   one hard to find

the wren on Snow White's finger sings:
    "in time   no america
        no countries at all
            a home among the bears
            honey and blackberries   all day long"
. . .

note for Snow White:
the smallest birds are always balanced
        on starvation's brink   their hunger requires
                continual effort
      no time to clean up your damn house
. . .

I guess I'll die without ever throwing
    a molotov cocktail at a bank or even
        just a martini into some annoying face

or learning the language of birds
so as to congratulate
    the ingenious crow
        building a nest
            of wire hangers

. . .

    the bluebird sings falsetto
        high and lonesome
            from the knife edge
                *can't find no heaven, don't care where they go**

---

* *This line is from* Hard Time Killin' Floor Blues, *by Skip James*

Wheel

After hungry ghosts come animals, then the human world. Why have we stopped? Has there been an accident, or is this the experience we paid for? Our gondola rocks at the apogee. Please be still, please don't overturn this creaky boat. The world falls away in all directions; the checkered map stretches toward mystery. The fair below is tiny, small as a nutshell. The wheel groans, sweet-sour music rising on the smell of burning sugar. Death gnaws the wheel: we are exactly between his fangs. Between the dizzy rise and fall, joy

Acknowledgements

I am grateful to the editors who published these poems in the following journals, sometimes in slightly different forms:

"Kawaii Killer" *Barrelhouse*
"Many Worlds Theory" *Bear Review*
"History" *Boston Hassle*
"Jerome in the Wilderness" *Cleaver*
"Not Working" *Epigraph*
"Wheel" *Eunoia*
"An Offering" *F(r)iction*
"No Rescue" "To Speak" "Him Again" and "Little House
    in the Forest of Giant Ferns" *Lily Poetry Review*
"Andromeda" and "Erinys" *Pangyrus*
"Like this, Like That" *RadarPoetry*
"When We Met" *Salamander*
"Penelope Unweaving" *Summer Stock*
"The Angel" *Tammy*
"Apophenia" *Tampa Review*

"Plague Diary" "Full Flower Moon" "Spring Moon" and "History" were included in Lily Poetry Review's anthology, *Voices Amidst the Virus: Poets Respond to the Pandemic*

"Psyche", "Cacoethes", and "Penelope Unweaving"also appeared in my chapbook, *Grandmother Mountain,* published by Blue Lyra Press as part of its Delphi Series.

Orginally from Detroit, by way of Boston, Martha McCollough now lives in Amherst, Massachusetts. She has an MFA in painting from Pratt Institute. Her chapbook, Grandmother Mountain, was published by Blue Lyra Press in October 2019

CPSIA information can be obtained
at www.ICGtesting.com
Printed in the USA
LVHW092040140222
711109LV00005B/265

9 781737 504351